HOW ECONOMICS WORKS

EARNING MONEY

By Patricia J. Murphy

Lerner Publications Company
Minneapolis

To my family for teaching me that the most
important things in life are FREE.
Love, PJM

Special thanks to Janet Bodnar, David S. Chernow, Dara Duguay, Doug Miller, Tom Ehrenfeld, Terry Savage, Allie and Maggie Cawood-Smith and family, Mary Catherine Lindsey and family, Evan and Elise Macmillan and family, and Devon Green and family.

Earning Money has been written solely to offer ideas to children about starting a moneymaking opportunity. This book does not make any claims or guarantees that its information will help a child actually earn money. The author and publisher take no responsibility or liability in the success or failure of moneymaking opportunities suggested by this book. When beginning a business, children and their parents should contact the appropriate city, state, and federal authorities for more specific information on regulations, taxes, permits, and licenses. For tax, legal, and safety matters, qualified experts should also be consulted. Good luck!

Lerner Publications Company
A division of Lerner Publishing Group
241 First Avenue North
Minneapolis, MN 55401 U.S.A.

Website address: www.lernerbooks.com

Library of Congress Cataloging-in-Publication Data

Murphy, Patricia J., 1963-
    Earning money / by Patricia J. Murphy.
      p.   cm. — (How economics works)
    Includes bibliographical references and index.
    ISBN-13: 978-0-8225-2149-5 (lib. bdg. : alk. paper)
    ISBN-10: 0-8225-2149-0 (lib. bdg. : alk. paper)
    1. Money-making projects for children—Juvenile literature. 2. Money—
Juvenile literature. 3. Children's allowances—Juvenile literature. 4. Work—
Juvenile literature. I. Title. II. Series.
    HF5392.M87 2006
    650.1'2'083—dc22   2004019712

Manufactured in the United States of America
1 2 3 4 5 6 – DP – 11 10 09 08 07 06

Table of Contents

Chapter 1
Money: Why Do We Need It? How Do We Make It?

Some people think a lot about money. Do you remember the first time you thought about it? Most likely, you first noticed money when you saw your mother or father use money to buy something. Or maybe they paid someone to repair the car or to cut the grass. One day you got your little mitts on some money. Your mother or father gave you money to buy something at a store. Maybe your grandparents gave you some money for your birthday. And money became a part of your life.

With each coin or bill, your generous relatives were teaching you about money. You learned that you could use it to buy candy, CDs, and movie tickets. Through the years, you've seen your parents and others make choices about spending money. Should they buy the big SUV (a want) or repair the family car (a need)? Money helps you buy both your wants and your needs.

What exactly are wants and needs? Wants are things you can live without but would like to have. These things are different for everyone. You may want a new pair of expensive sneakers. Your friend might want a new video game. Needs are things people cannot live without. Food, clothes, and a place to live would be on everyone's list of needs. To meet your wants and needs, you need money. How do you get the money you need?

MONEY FOR PRODUCTS AND SERVICES

Money doesn't just fly out of automated teller machines (ATMs), grow on trees, or magically appear behind your

VALUE ADDED

Bills (paper money) of the lowest value change hands more often than bills of higher value. Here's how long the typical bill lasts before wearing out:

$1 bill: 22 months	$10 bill: 18 months	$50 bill: 5 years
$5 bill: 16 months	$20 bill: 2 years	$100 bill: 8.5 years

ears. Money usually has to be earned. Your parents have had to work to earn money. This work was either making something (a product) or doing something (a service) for other people. And people were willing to pay your parents money for the product or service.

People pay for products and services every day. Products are things you can touch or hold. Products include things like food, CDs, clothes, and cars. Services include acts, such as selling houses, paving driveways, and repairing cars or bikes. When people trade their money for a product or a service, they are saying, "What you have is as valuable to me as this money I hold." They exchange, or trade, their money for something another person has or can do for them. Most people work for money. They use the money they earn for the products and services they need or want.

WHERE DOES MONEY COME FROM?

The money that people work so hard for gets a workout. Money moves from hand to hand for a long time. The coin you picked up off the ground yesterday could be nearly thirty years old. Paper money wears out sooner than coins, but it can also last many years.

Bills (paper money) stay in use until they are worn out or badly torn. Then banks exchange their old bills and coins for brand new ones. Banks send old bills to the Federal Reserve

BANK ON IT In just one day, the Bureau of Engraving and Printing makes 37 million bills with a total value of about $696 million.

System. The Federal Reserve is the central bank of the United States. Workers there shred old bills and recycle or bury them. Old coins go to the U.S. Mint. Workers melt down old coins and use the metal again to make shiny, new coins.

Two U.S. Treasury Department agencies can make money. They are the Bureau of Engraving and Printing and the U.S. Mint. The Bureau of Engraving and Printing makes paper money. The mint makes coins. You can visit these places to watch dollar bills and coins being made— but you won't get any free samples. Mints in Denver,

A worker inspects the series 2001 one-dollar bills at the Bureau of Engraving and Printing in Washington, D.C.

The Federal Reserve Bank in Minneapolis, Minnesota, is one of twelve banks in the Federal Reserve System.

Colorado, and Philadelphia, Pennsylvania, make most of the coins people use. Mints in San Francisco, California, and West Point, New York, make coins to mark special occasions. The Bureau of Engraving and Printing is in Washington, D.C.

HOW DO YOU GET YOUR HANDS ON SOME MONEY?

With all this talk about money, you're probably wondering, "How can I get some?" Well, you've come to the right place. In these pages, you'll find some thoughts, ideas, tips, and answers to questions that can help you earn money.

You might not start a business out of your garage like Microsoft's computer wizard Bill Gates did. But you will learn a thing or two about earning money.

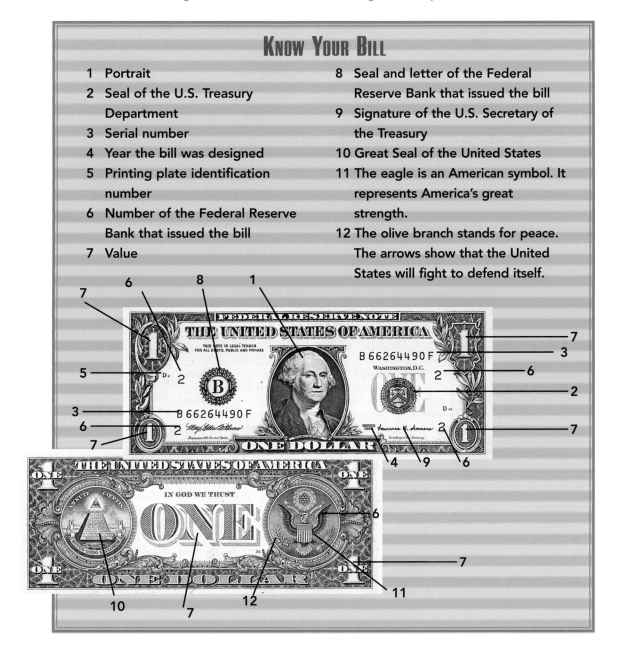

KNOW YOUR BILL

1 Portrait
2 Seal of the U.S. Treasury Department
3 Serial number
4 Year the bill was designed
5 Printing plate identification number
6 Number of the Federal Reserve Bank that issued the bill
7 Value

8 Seal and letter of the Federal Reserve Bank that issued the bill
9 Signature of the U.S. Secretary of the Treasury
10 Great Seal of the United States
11 The eagle is an American symbol. It represents America's great strength.
12 The olive branch stands for peace. The arrows show that the United States will fight to defend itself.

CHAPTER 2
ALLOW ME:
GETTING AN ALLOWANCE

Webster's dictionary defines the word *allowance* as "a sum given in return for expenses." For most tweens, an allowance is another name for money, dough, cash, or income given to them by their parents. Some kids get an allowance for doing chores around the house or keeping up good grades. Others get an allowance for nothing at all.

According to the Yankelovich Youth Monitor, a study of kids done for America's top five hundred companies,

56 percent of tweens (ages nine to eleven) and 67 percent of teens (ages twelve to fourteen) get some kind of allowance. The average pay is somewhere between $8.00 and $11.30 per week. Sounds like a pretty good deal, huh? Well, it only gets better. Since most teens don't have any big bills to pay, this money often pays for F-U-N.

ASKING FOR AN ALLOWANCE

If you don't already get an allowance, ask for one. With an allowance, you can start stashing cash for a rainy day—or for rainy-day fun. You can save for trips to museums or ball games or for the latest CDs, DVDs, or video games.

BOTTOM LINE
You can fold a dollar bill four thousand times before it tears.

If you need some help to convince your parents that you need an allowance, try these two points:

(1) Money experts agree that an allowance helps teach tweens how to handle their own money.
(2) You'll stop hounding your parents for money every time you want to buy or do something. HONEST.

Can you already hear the opening of Dad's wallet or Mom's purse? Well, just hold on to your piggy banks for a minute. Here are a few surefire ways to talk to your parents about an allowance.

LET'S TALK ALLOWANCE—YOURS!

First, do your homework. Make a list of the things you need each week, why you need them, and how much they cost. Make sure to list the costs of your hobbies, holiday and birthday gifts, and snacks.

Then get to the point. Say, "Mom and Dad, I would like to receive an allowance." You'll be surprised how easy it is to convince them.

Explain why you need an allowance. Be honest. State the reasons you want an allowance. Talk about your expenses and what you want to pay for with your allowance. Then talk about how much money you think you need and how often you hope to be paid.

Discuss what you may (or may not) do in return. Most parents like the idea of tweens earning an allowance. They believe that earning money teaches tweens the value of hard work. Many parents also think that an allowance shows tweens how the real world works. When people work, they earn money. It's that simple. Or is it?

VALUE ADDED

Expecting BIG BILLS in your future? Then you'll want to know how to tell them apart. Match the statesmen to the bills on which their faces are printed. Answers are on page 20. No peeking!

1. $1	Ulysses S. Grant
2. $2	Abraham Lincoln
3. $5	Thomas Jefferson
4. $10	Benjamin Franklin
5. $20	Alexander Hamilton
6. $50	Andrew Jackson
7. $100	George Washington

Other parents have different views. Some don't mind giving their kids money without them having to earn it. And some parents think teens and tweens should help around the house without pay. After all, they are part of the family. They live in the same house and should help keep it neat and clean. What do you think? Be prepared to talk about chores you can help with around the house in exchange for an allowance.

Finally, shake on it. Whatever deal you and your parents strike, make it official. Shake on it. Sign a paper. Draw up a chart. Include what has to be done and when. That way, there won't be any questions or arguments. And you'll soon be reaping the benefits of an allowance.

BANK ON IT A dollar bill is 2.61 inches high by 6.14 inches wide by .0043 inch thick.

Asking for a Raise

If you already receive an allowance, it may be time to ask for a raise. Follow the steps above. You may also want to think of ways you could earn the extra money.

Need even more money? Want to earn some money on your own? Then read on. The next four chapters of this book are sure to give you an idea or two (or three) for earning money. Believe it or not, inside YOU, there's a moneymaking machine. In fact, your machine might make so much money that you won't need an allowance anymore. So what are you waiting for? Turn the page. Start earning money!

CHAPTER 3
BRAINSTORMING A MONEYMAKING OPPORTUNITY

To brainstorm a possible moneymaking opportunity (MMO), you will want to open your mind. Find a quiet, safe place where your brain can fill with clouds of ideas, the wind can blow them around, and you can let your ideas rain down.

To get just the right conditions for your moneymaking brainstorm, here are a few buckets (or questions) to think about. The buckets will collect your ideas.

BUCKET 1: WHAT DO YOU LIKE TO DO?

What are your interests? The great Italian artist Michelangelo was interested in painting and sculpting. Famous electricity inventor Thomas A. Edison was interested in machines and electricity. Whatever work you choose, your success will depend on how interested you are in what you do. If you like doing something, you'll most likely keep doing it—and even try to get better at it.

Business sections of newspapers and magazines are filled with news about entrepreneurs (people who start their own businesses). And they all share one thing. They share a great love or enthusiasm for what they do. You can bet your sneakers that Yao Ming loves basketball, that Jessica Simpson loves to sing, and that computer genius Bill Gates and computers still click.

Your turn: Get a pencil. Make a list of all the things you like to do.

MONEY TALK Confucius (551–479 B.C.), a great Chinese teacher and thinker, once said, "Choose a job you love and you'll never have to work a day in your life." Can you imagine that?

BUCKET 2: WHAT ARE YOU REALLY GOOD AT?

Spill it. Don't be shy. You are one of a kind. There will never ever be anyone exactly like you (even if you're an identical twin). Your interests, talents, and skills are unique to you. Let your ideas flow. "Don't rule out something that you like to do—that you could be better at," says Tom Ehrenfeld, business writer and author of *The Start-Up Garden.* "You can always learn more skills."

Your turn: List your talents and skills. Draw a circle around your top five.

BUCKET 3: WHAT NEEDS
DO YOUR FAMILY, FRIENDS, OR NEIGHBORS HAVE?

Look. Listen. Sniff around. Ask questions. Are there things you could make or do for family, friends, or neighbors? Keep your eyes and ears peeled for opportunities. Read your local newspaper. Take walks around the block. What do you notice? Do you spy any needs that are not being met? Are there opportunities staring you in the face? It's time to do something about them.

"Take advantage of needs and opportunities, like selling refreshments and cookies at a yard sale or snacks at your neighborhood pool. They can be simple things," says Janet Bodnar.

MMO/BIZ Ideas

Talents/Skills	Needs/Opportunities	MMO/BIZ Idea
Sports (basketball, soccer)	Lots of kids in area, spring vacation, summertime	Sports camp, sports practice, lessons
Cooking, baking	Hungry people, garage sales, baseball games	Bake sales, baked goods company, lemonade stand
Writing stories, poems, ads	Magazines, local businesses, neighborhood organizations	Freelance writing, write for kids magazines and local businesses
Good at school	Kids who need help with schoolwork	Tutor kids at home or at the library
Love arts and crafts: jewelry, T-shirts, pottery, handbags, ornaments	Garage sales, art fairs, craft lovers, quick gifts	Sell crafts at sales, fairs, or in own business
Good with kids	Lots of kids in area	Babysitting; party, play group, or park helper
Holiday nut	Busy people who need holiday decorating, wrapping, gift ideas	Start decorating, holiday wrapping, and gift shopping biz
Good with pets	People with pet needs	Grooming, watching, walking, pet sitting

Bodnar is an expert on kids and money and the author of *Dollars & $ense for Kids.*

Finding these things will take some time in the rain. Don't be afraid to get wet! (That's what happens in a brainstorm!) Soon enough, it just may start raining dollars and cents.

Your turn: Keep a list of the needs and opportunities you discover. Next, see if any of your interests and talents match the needs and opportunities that you listed. Some probably will.

BUCKET 4: DO YOU HAVE BIG IDEAS, OR DO YOU LIKE TO INVENT THINGS?

Like twin sisters Allie and Maggie Cawood-Smith from Auburn, California, you might be one idea or invention away from something big. When Allie and Maggie were nine years old, they wanted to wear

Allie *(left)* and Maggie Cawood-Smith *(right)* make and sell their own lip balm.

lipstick. Their mother said, "Only if you make it!" With the help of their mother, who is also an herbalist (someone who collects and grows herbs), Allie and Maggie set out to make lipstick. They gathered lip-healing herbs from their garden and red beets to add color.

"When we mixed all the ingredients, we got red from the beets everywhere but in our lipstick. We ended up with a lip balm instead of lipstick!" says Maggie. Soon afterward, Allie and Maggie started wearing their lip balm and giving it as gifts. Then one day, they got an unBEETable idea.

ALLIE AND MAGGIE'S "UNBEETABLE" BIZ TIPS:

1. DO what you love, and the money will follow.
2. DO check out stores, mail-order catalogs, newspapers, magazines, and the Internet. See if someone is already making what you want to make (or sell) or offering the service that you want to offer. Make sure that your product or service will be well received.
3. DO make a plan and set goals.
4. DO go into business for yourself, because YOU want to do it.
5. DON'T get burned out. Get away from the business from time to time. Your MMO should add to your life—not take away from it.
6. DO whatever you want to do! The sky's the limit. If we can do it, you can too.

"Maggie's cello teacher said that we should sell it!" said Allie. And that's just what they did. With a little money from their mother, word-of-mouth advertising, store-to-store selling, hand-painted tins, and a website designed by dear Uncle Dave, Beet Lips was born. Fast-forward six years. Allie and Maggie, by then fifteen, were still in business. Their lip balm business allowed them to learn about both herbs and business, while they earned extra spending money, saved for college, and invested in the stock market (kids under the age of eighteen may only invest in the stock market with the help of an adult). "Having Beet Lips has given me the ability to create something," says Maggie, "and to believe that I can do anything that I put my mind to."

Your turn: What are you waiting for?

ANSWERS FOR GAME ON PAGE 12

1. George Washington
2. Thomas Jefferson
3. Abraham Lincoln
4. Alexander Hamilton
5. Andrew Jackson
6. Ulysses S. Grant
7. Benjamin Franklin

CHAPTER 4
PLANNING A MONEYMAKING OPPORTUNITY

With your brainstormed ideas close at hand, think about how your interests, talents, skills, needs, and opportunities might translate into a MMO plan.

To start planning, you'll first need to answer some key questions: What? Why? Who? How? Where? When? Your thoughtful answers will help you plan your MMO. So let's go.

What? What do you want to do—make a product or offer a service? Look back at your lists of interests, talents, and needs for ideas, and check out the MMO Ideas list (on page 17) for other suggestions. "But don't bite off more than you can chew,"

warns author Janet Bodnar. "Kids who make it in business ask for help from their families, don't require much start up money, are close to their homes—and most are *service* businesses."

Why? What is the real reason you want to start your own MMO? While some entrepreneurs get into business for the money, it's not always the reason they stay in business.

"Growing a business grows you," says author Tom Ehrenfeld. "Your business will help you do something you believe in while helping others, allow you to create something to care about—that is uniquely YOU—and reward you for what you're good at!"

Who? Who is going into business? Are you doing this alone, or do you have a partner? Will you seek the help of your parents or an expert in your new field? Who will your customers be?

How? How will you make your product or offer your service? Do you have the cooking skills to make Grandma's super-duper, double-decker fudge? Are your handmade craft items ready for the market? You may want to make a batch or two (or three) of Grandma's fudge or take another class before you begin your business. Having the skills to offer a top-notch product or service will set you apart from the ordinary bake sale and craft bunch.

REACHING YOUR CUSTOMERS

Should you make a flyer or brochure, design a website, or rely on word-of-mouth advertising to let your customers know about your business? Allie and Maggie Cawood-Smith did all of the above, just not all at once. The twins started out slowly. First, they sold their lip balm out of their house. Then they asked stores to sell their product. Soon they followed up with a website.

Allie and Maggie's website *(left)* helped boost sales of their popular Beet Lips lip balm *(logo below)*.

Allie and Maggie quickly learned that the more they sold, the more they could sell. "Once we started selling our product, people loved it and kept ordering more and more. It was word-of-mouth advertising that has kept our sales going!" said Maggie.

Happy customers will be your best advertising. They will tell others about your product or service and help create more happy customers. To get your first happy customers, however, you'll have to spread the word with flyers.

Your first flyers don't have to be fancy. They just have to be eye-catching and have the right information. Flyers can be computer-generated or handwritten with your name, your product or service, and your phone number or e-mail address. Remember, well-made flyers will show possible customers that you mean business.

Once you've got your flyers made, start mailing them to your family and friends and handing them out in your neighborhood and at special events. Ask store owners to hang the flyers in their stores. Then think of other places where you can spread the word. Arm yourself with flyers and go there. Ask others to help.

Once you get customers, you'll have to work hard to keep them. The secret? Keep them happy. To keep your customers smiling, ask them from time to time, "How am I doing?" Listen to both the positive and negative comments. They will help you to become better at your business and to offer a better product or service.

Spread the Word (How to Find Customers)

Drum up some business with a bright, well-written flyer, brochure, website, business card, or all of the above. Whatever pieces you choose to make, be sure to include the following parts:

- Headline in **BIG BOLD LETTERS**
- Graphic, picture, or a drawing of you or your product
- List of reasons for using your product or service
- Your name, phone number, address, and e-mail
- A snappy tagline, or slogan— something to help customers remember you and your product or service

Here's a flyer for Grace Burke's cat-sitting service:

AMAZING GRACE'S CAT-SITTING SERVICE

I am sweet, reliable, and great with cats

Can sit afternoons, evenings, and special occasions

Will provide food, water, and tender, loving care

Will clean litter box

References available upon request

Call Grace Burke (555) 455-2343

"Cats think she's amazing!"
—Grace's grandmother and cat owner

Running your own business is a lot of work, but it can also be very fun and rewarding, as Elise and Evan Macmillan demonstrate above.

Where? Where will you do this service or make this product? You'll probably want to set aside a space to run your MMO—a desk, part of your bedroom, or part of your parents' garage. Think about the supplies and tools you'll need and where you can store them.

When? When will you make your products or offer your service? There are only twenty-four hours in a day. You also have school, friends, and family events to think about. Decide how much time you want to put into your MMO. Sure, you'll have to put time into it, but make sure to balance it with the rest of your life.

HOW ABOUT A BUSINESS CARD?

Want to pass out business cards too? Print the name of your business, your name, your tagline, and your phone number on small cards. See Grace's sample business card:

AMAZING GRACE'S CAT-SITTING SERVICE

Grace Burke
(555) 455-2343

"Cats think she's amazing!"
—Grace's grandmother and cat owner

Evan and Elise's Chocolate
Farm website

Your turn: Try your hand at a simple MMO plan. Start by answering the questions in this chapter. Need some encouragement? Listen to this! Fifteen-year-old Evan Macmillan and his thirteen-year-old sister, Elise, wrote their first business plan when they started the Chocolate Farm in Denver, Colorado. They made chocolate in the shapes of farm animals, such as cows, horses, and pigs. They sold their first chocolate animals at a holiday marketplace. Since then, Evan and Elise have added to and changed their first business plan. "We've learned by doing," says Elise, "and by always thinking BIG. If you do, you'll never know what will happen!" Elise and Evan have created one of the top youth food companies in the United States.

CHAPTER 5:
STARTING A
MONEYMAKING OPPORTUNITY

Whether you want to make a product or offer a service, you've got to jump right in and do it. You've brainstormed a bit and thought about a plan. What's next? It's time to begin. Here are a few things to think about as you start your business.

DO YOUR BEST!

Your product or service must be the BEST you can offer. Put in time and make your best effort. If your MMO is not worth your best effort, why bother to do it? Think about it. If you don't put your best effort into your business, your product or service won't be any good and you won't have any customers. "Nothing beats a quality product or service and pleasing your customers," says Doug Miller of the Kauffman Center of Entrepreneurial Leadership in Kansas City, Missouri.

MAKE MISTAKES

When starting your new business, you're bound to make some mistakes. Give yourself permission to make them. Mistakes can be turned into valuable lessons. Many successful businesspeople think of mistakes or failures as learning opportunities and chances to try again.

Elise Macmillan and her brother, Evan, learned valuable lessons from mistakes they made when their business was new. "When we started sending our chocolates all over, we learned that chocolate melts *really* easily. So we started

using ice packs. We made a mistake—and then made a change that helped our business!" says Elise.

ASK FOR HELP

Mistakes can help. So can family members and friends—if you let them. With the help of her parents, thirteen-year-old Mary Catherine Lindsay of Atlanta, Georgia, turned a school project into a stationery design company called Grasshopper Press. She knew she was on to something when she sold her stationery at school. Mary Catherine earned more than eight hundred dollars the very first day. Soon she had a booth at the Atlanta Gift Show. Then she started selling her stationery—which comes in more than two hundred designs—to several stores. It's hopping off shelves and being sold on the Internet. And it all started by asking her parents for help. "Don't be afraid to ask for help from family, friends, and especially your parents," says

MONEY TALK "Failure is the chance to begin again more intelligently." —Henry Ford, founder of the Ford Motor Company

Grasshopper Press®

With the help of her parents, Mary Catherine Lindsay turned her talent for making stationery into a booming stationery business called Grasshopper Press *(logo above).*

Mary Catherine. "If you don't know something or realize that you can't do something your-self, ask for help. It's no big deal. It's part of life."

BE HONEST

Being honest is also a part of life. You've probably heard the old saying "Honesty is the best poli-cy." It's the best business policy too. To succeed in business, you must say what you mean, mean what you say, and stand by your word. Your word needs to mean something. Tom Ehrenfeld suggests, "Be honest, be fair, do what you say, and be mindful of others. The same rules in life apply in business."

BANK ON IT First Lady Martha Washington (1731–1802) is the only woman to appear on U.S. paper money. Her face appeared on the paper one-dollar silver certificate in 1886, 1891, and 1898. Silver certificates could be exchanged for silver coins.

Doug Miller agrees. "Remember that your business goals should never be more important than your values," he says. "It doesn't matter how much money you make if you break values." Everyone knows that cheating on tests, lying to friends, and breaking promises are bad things to do. Well, the same goes for business practices. You should never cheat, lie, or break promises you make to your customers. It's not only wrong—in the business world, it's also illegal.

BE INVENTIVE

Businesspeople are always trying to invent new products and services to sell. That makes things more interesting and increases sales. Remember Allie and Maggie Cawood-Smith? After doing some research, they found that there were few products for people with body art. So they are expanding their product line with another balm for tattoos and body piercings. Allie and Maggie plan to call their new body balm Steel Heal.

Chocolate Farm's Elise and Evan Macmillan received lots of requests from customers who wanted to learn how to make their own chocolates. The Macmillans met their customers' needs by offering chocolate-making kits, supplies, and cookbooks.

WORK HARD

Both Allie and Maggie Cawood-Smith's and Elise and Evan Macmillan's big ideas came from hard work. They did the necessary research and listened to their customers. You, too, will have to work hard to become as successful as they are. "We live in a country where if you work hard, you can make money, be independent, and be successful," says David S. Chernow, president and chief executive officer (CEO) of Junior Achievement, Inc., an organization that teaches kids about money and business.

GIVE BACK

Many successful businesspeople give back to their communities. They

MONEY Makers Inventor Thomas Edison (1847–1931) once said, "I've not failed. I have just found 10,000 ways that won't work." With that attitude, Edison went on to invent the lightbulb, talking pictures (movies), the phonograph (record player), and more than one thousand other devices!

donate their time and money to help the earth and the people on it. Twelve-year-old Devon Green's business, Devon's Heal the World Recycling of Stuart, Florida, is all about giving back. Her company collects pounds and pounds of aluminum cans and other recyclable goods. Each week Devon and her father take the "recycling trailer," pulled by the family van, to more than one hundred area homes and businesses. Then Devon trades the goods for money at a recycling center. With the money she earns, she pays herself and gives 30 percent of her earnings to charity. Her reason? "If you own your business and give back to your community, you will always get back ten times more than you gave as long as your heart is in the right place," says Devon.

Through Devon's business, she's been able to save money for her future and help people and animals in need. She's also received a variety of honors, attention from newspapers and TV shows, and a feeling that she's making a difference in the world.

DOLLARS & SENSE Franklin D. Roosevelt (1882–1945), the thirty-second president of the United States, said, "Happiness lies not in the mere possession of money, it lies in the joy of achievement, in the thrill of the creative effort."

Devon Green helps heal the earth
through her recycling business.

Some would call Devon a "social entrepreneur." That's because she's making money and helping society and the environment. But whatever you call her, she's trying to do what founding father and inventor Ben Franklin tried to do—"to do well by doing good."

HAVE FUN

Devon has fun helping the earth, and she also makes money at it. Your MMO should be fun too. If you're not having fun, you might get bored and not keep working at your MMO. If and when that happens, look at your ideas list and think of something else that you enjoy doing. If you like what you're doing, keep doing it. If not, try something new. "Try different things to help you decide," says Doug Miller. "Knowing what you don't want to do is just as important as knowing what you do."

CHAPTER 6:
KEEPING TRACK
OF YOUR EARNINGS

While you're brainstorming, planning, and starting your MMO, you'll also want to think of ways to keep track of your earnings. Record keeping and budgeting are important business tools. To keep close track of your MMO, use either a notebook, note cards, or your family computer. Here are steps to get you started.

MAKE AND KEEP RECEIPTS
Whether you're earning money by making cookies or teaching someone how to use a computer, you will need to

record every sale. With each sale, write a receipt—a record of the sale—with the name of your customer, the date the sale was made, the amount of the sale, and what was sold. You may want to purchase receipt pads with carbon paper from an office supply store. These will allow you to keep copies of the receipts you give to your customers.

EXPENSES

What about expenses—the costs of running your business? Expenses include things like the cost of paper and ink cartridges for printing your flyers, ingredients for making cookies—whatever you need to buy to run your business. When you buy your supplies, the cashier will give you a receipt, a record of the sale. The receipt shows how much money you paid. Keep all your receipts. On these receipts, write down what you bought. Keep copies of the receipts you give your customers in one shoe box and the receipts you receive for

Receipt 1	Date: 5/28
For: 6 cookies at 50¢ each	To: Mr. Chip
Total cost: $3.00	*Thank you for your sweet business! Erik*
Cash received: $3.00	
Change due: $0.00	
Receipt 2	Date: May 29
For: 2 hours of computer	To: Mr. Byte
lessons at $4.00 an hour.	*Thank you for computing with me! Olivia*
Total cost: $8.00	
Cash received: $10.00	
Change due: $2.00	

your expenses in another shoe box. Carefully saved, these receipts will be proof of your incoming and outgoing money—your income and your expenses.

RECORD THE RECEIPTS

In a notebook, index card, or computer, record all your receipts for income and expenses. For sales (income), write down the date, the amount of the sale, and the name and address of your customers.

MY EARNINGS:

Date	Amount of Sale	Customer's Name	Address
5/2	$ 8.00 (2 hours)	Mr. Byte	1234 Help Me Lane
5/15	$16.00 (4 hours)	Mr. Mouse	5678 I Get It Now Street
5/26	$32.00 (8 hours)	Mr. Web	101112 Worldwide Drive
5/27	$ 4.00 (1 hour)	Ms. Button	131415 First Timer Blvd.
5/20	$ 4.00 (1 hour)	Mr. Switch	161718 Turned It on Road
May Total:	$ 64 (16 hours)	5 customers	

Do the same thing for your expenses. Record what you purchased and the amount paid.

At the end of the week (or month), add the sales to see how much you earned. Next, add the expenses to see how much you spent. Then subtract the expenses from the sales to find out what your profit is. Your profit is the amount of money that's left from your earnings after all the expenses have been paid.

		MY EXPENSES:					
Date		**Item/Use**		**Amount**			
5/3		Computer discs for saving work		$13.00			
5/11		Computer paper for flyers, etc.		$ 6.00			
5/12		New computer how-to book		$12.00			
5/26		New stapler for office		$ 5.00			
May Total:		**May expenses**		**$36.00**			

If you're making a profit or breaking even (your sales equal your expenses), congratulations! If you don't make a profit, you might want to think of ways to cut down on expenses or charge more for your product or service. But with this added cost to your customers, you'll want to add value. Most people won't pay more if they're not getting more. You may also just want to give your new MMO more time to grow. As more people hear about your business and the good job you're doing, sales are likely to increase.

"Don't get discouraged," says David S. Chernow. "Some ideas may fail, some may succeed. Realize that you are learning and appreciate the successes and failures. Losing is part of the journey. Success is in the trying."

CREATING A BUDGET

A budget is a plan of what you'll do with the money you earn. How much will you save? How much will you spend? What money will you put aside

DOLLARS & SENSE "Many of life's failures are people who did not realize how close they were to success when they gave up." —Thomas A. Edison, inventor

to keep your MMO going?

"A budget lets you live within your means, lets you make decisions, and manage your own money," says Dara Duguay, executive director of the Jump$tart Coalition for Personal Financial Literacy in Washington, D.C. "Making choices with your own money takes time. With someone else's money, your choices seem unlimited."

See for yourself. Spending your hard-earned money takes longer than spending money someone just gives to you. Why? Because you've learned firsthand how hard it is to make a buck. You won't part with it so quickly.

To start your budget, label a section in your record-keeping

THE STORY OF THE $ SIGN

The dollar sign ($) may have a Mexican or Spanish origin. It's believed that long ago, people in Mexico and Spain wrote P[s] in front of numbers used to indicate an amount of money. The P[s] was a short way to write pesos, the word for certain Spanish coins. For example, P[s]3 was short for three pesos. If you were hand-writing P[s] fast—because it's part of a long document you're working on—you might join the letters, so they might look like this $. If you shorten the P to a single stroke, then the letters become one, creating a $ symbol. The $ symbol first appeared in the 1770s in documents of British Americans who did business with Spanish Americans. It appeared in print after 1800.

system "My Budget." This is where you will decide what to do with your profits. Sure, a few purchases might come to mind, such as a big pepperoni pizza or the shoes you've had your eyes on. How you spend your profits is up to you. But before you blow your hard-earned cash, you might want to think about saving and setting some goals.

SAVING AND SETTING GOALS

Author Janet Bodnar suggests that you "save at least half of everything you make. Use some of the money to buy things you need for your business, and what's left over could be used for spending money. If you don't do this, all of the money will slip through your fingertips."

To ensure that your income does not go slip-sliding away, Paul Lermitte, in his book *Making Allowances: Dollars and Sense,* suggests setting goals. He sets some short-term, medium-term, and long-term savings goals. You may want to write down your goals in the budget section of your notebook or computer file.

Short-term savings goals would be for things you'd like to have right away—like a hot dog for lunch or a pack of gum. Medium-term savings goals might be items that you'd like to buy soon, but they will take a few weeks or months to save for. They will cost more than your short-term savings goals. These items might include a new snowboard or a fancy pair of shoes. Long-term savings goals would be larger, more costly items for your future, such as a car or your college education.

WILL I HAVE TO PAY TAXES?

If you earn more than $400 in one year, you will owe self-employment taxes. If you earn more than $4,750, you'll have to file an income tax return. (This form records and reports your earnings to the government.) Most tweens who run businesses won't have to worry about either. To find out if you will, keep track of your income and check with the Internal Revenue Service (IRS). The IRS is the part of the U.S. Treasury Department that collects taxes. For the most up-to-date figures and rules that might apply to your MMO, go to http://www.irs.gov.

Want another idea? Terry Savage, money expert and author of *Savage on Money,* suggests a challenge. "For every dollar you choose to save, ask your parents to add two dollars—and put it into a bank account or a money market account (savings accounts in which your money earns money). Then by the time you're ready for college, half of your earnings can go toward paying for college— the other half you could divide up for other things that you'll need."

But whatever you do, it's YOUR choice. It needs to be. While this new money of yours probably won't make you happier, your new spending power will let you be more independent and give you the power to make more choices. And if you choose wisely, you'll have the power to make a lot of good things happen inside you and in the world around you.

Money through the Years

Money has not always been handy coins and bills. It has changed shape through the years. Here are a few examples:

9000–6000 B.C. People traded cows, sheep, and camels for goods and services. People traded for all sorts of things, including shells, tea leaves, feathers, animal teeth, blankets, and barley.

1200 B.C. People used cowrie shells, the shells of sea animals, as money.

1000 B.C. The Chinese made round coins out of bronze, copper, and other metals. Some people used bars of valuable metals, weapons, tools, and ornaments as money.

500 B.C. Greek, Turkish, Persian, and Macedonian people made coins out of silver, bronze, and gold.

A.D. 806 The Chinese printed the world's first paper money.

1535 In North America, early European settlers and Native Americans traded wampum, strings of beads made from shells.

1700 Early European settlers in North America brought their own money to the American colonies. Some Virginia and Maryland farmers traded the tobacco they grew to buy the things they needed.

1787 The first U.S. coin was made of silver.

1792 The first U.S. mint opened in Philadelphia, Pennsylvania.

1861 The U.S. government issued its first paper money, called legal tender notes, or U.S. notes.

1996 The United States began issuing newly designed paper money, starting with the $100 bill.

GLOSSARY

advertising: information shared publicly about something that you want to sell

automated teller machines (ATMs): machines that people use to make deposits to, withdrawals from, or payment transfers between their bank accounts

brainstorm: to think of ideas or solutions to a problem

entrepreneur: someone who starts his or her own business

expenses: the costs of running a business

income: money that someone earns or receives regularly

income tax: a payment made to the government based on the amount of money a person makes

money market: a special savings account that earns money called interest

profit: the amount of money left over after all of the costs of running a business are subtracted from the money earned

receipts: records of sales. A receipt shows how much money you paid for a product or service.

save: to keep money to use in the future instead of spending it immediately

Source Notes

15   Confucius, Bartleby.com, http://www.bartleby.com/66/86/13086.html (March 11, 2005).

15–16   Tom Ehrenfeld, telephone conversation with author, February 12, 2003.

16   Janet Bodnar, telephone conversation with author, April 3, 2003.

19   Maggie Cawood-Smith, telephone conversation with author, April 26, 2003.

20   Allie Cawood-Smith, telephone conversation with author, April 26, 2003.

20   Maggie Cawood-Smith, telephone conversation.

22   Bodnar, telephone conversation.

22   Ehrenfeld, telephone conversation.

24   Maggie Cawood-Smith, telephone conversation.

27   Elise and Evan Macmillan, telephone conversation with author, March 16, 2003.

29–30   Ibid.

30   Henry Ford, The Quotations Page, n.d. http://www.quotationspage.com/quote/33629.html> (March 11, 2005).

30–31   Mary Catherine Lindsay, telephone conversation with author, February 25, 2003.

31   Ehrenfeld, telephone conversation.

31   Doug Miller, telephone conversation with author, March 28, 2003.

32   Thomas Edison, wikiquote.org, December 12, 2004, http://en.wikiquote.org/wiki/Thomas_Edison (March 11, 2005).

32   David S. Chernow, telephone conversation with author, February 4, 2003.

33   Devon Green, telephone conversation with author, April 8, 2003.

33   Conrad Black, *Franklin Delano Roosevelt: Champion of Freedom* (New York: Public Affairs, 2003), 271.

34   Ben Franklin, *Poor Richard's Almanack* (Philadelphia: B. Franklin, 1733) as referenced in *Ben Franklin: An American Life* (New York: W. Issacson, 2003) p. 94.

34   Miller, telephone conversation.

38   Chernow, telephone conversation.

38   Thomas Edison, wikiquote.org.

39   Dara Duguay, telephone conversation with author, March 19, 2003.

40   Bodnar, telephone conversation.

41   Terry Savage, telephone interview with author, March 23, 2003.

SELECTED BIBLIOGRAPHY

BOOKS

Bodnar, Janet. *Mom, Can I Have This?* New York: Kiplinger Times Business, 1996.

Ehrenfeld, Tom. *The Start-Up Garden: How Growing a Business Grows You.* New York: McGraw-Hill, 2002.

Feigenbaum, Alan. *Parent's Guide to Money: Raising Financially Savvy Children.* Los Angeles: Parent's Guide Press, 2002.

Lermitte, Paul W. *Making Allowances: Dollars and Sense.* New York: McGraw-Hill Books, 2002.

Mariotti, Steve. *The Young Entrepreneur's Guide to Starting and Running a Business.* New York: Kiplinger Times Business, 1996.

Searls, Michael J. *How to Make Money Make Sense to Your Kids.* New York: Summit Financial Publishing, 1998.

Vallee, Danielle. *Whiz Teens in Business: Enjoy Yourself While Making Money.* Kansas City, MO: Truman Publishing Co., 1999.

WEBSITES

Build: Businesses United in Investing, Lending, and Development (BUILD)
http://www.build.org
BUILD is a nonprofit organization for teens working to build economic opportunities.

Kauffman Center for Entrepreneurial Leadership
http://www.entreworld.org
This site is the ultimate resource center (online and in Kansas City, MO) for entrepreneurs around the word. The site also has a young-entrepreneur section.

National Foundation for Teaching Entrepreneurship
http://www.nfte.com
This home website for the NFTE offers programs on teaching entrepreneurship to teens and tweens.

The Startup Garden Website
http://www.startupgarden.com
This is the website of Tom Ehrenfeld, the author of *The Start-Up Garden.* Ehrenfeld offers additional pieces of advice, strategy, and inspiration for people wishing to start a new company.

The U.S. Bureau of Engraving and Printing
http://www.moneyfactory.gov
This is the U.S. Treasury Department's website for the Bureau of Engraving and Printing. The website includes information on paper money—from the latest issues to fun facts for kids.

The U.S. Mint
http://www.usmint.gov and http://www.usmint.gov/kids
The official website for the U.S. Treasury Department includes information on the U.S. Mint, the U.S. Bureau of Engraving and Printing, and the Internal Revenue Service. It includes the latest information on coins and a link for fun facts for kids.

U.S. Small Business Administration
http://www.sba.gov
Get information on starting, financing, and managing small business opportunities in the United States.

The U.S. Treasury Department
http://www.ustreas.gov
This is the official website for the U.S. Treasury Department (USTD). The website includes information on the U.S. Mint, the U.S. Bureau Engraving and Printing, and the Internal Revenue Service. The website offers Treasury Department news, press releases, and direct links to find the USTD's latest information.

FURTHER READING AND WEBSITES

BOOKS

Berg, Adrienne, and Arthur Berg Bochner. *The Totally Awesome Business Book for Kids.* New York: Newmarket Press, 2002.

Blume, Judy. *Double Fudge.* New York: Dutton Children's Books, 2002.

Bodnar, Janet. *Dollars & $ense for Kids.* New York: Random House, 2003.

Hershenhorn, Esther. *The Confessions and Secrets of Howard J. Fingerhut.* New York: Holiday House, 2002.

McCloskey, Robert. *Homer Price.* New York: The Viking Press, 1971.

McQuinn, Conn. *KidsBiz: Everything You Need to Start Your Own Business.* New York: Puffin Books, 1999.

Viorst, Judith. *Alexander, Who Used to Be Rich Last Sunday.* New York: Atheneum, 1985.

WEBSITES

Entrepreneurship Education on the Web
http://www.eweb.slu.edu/youth_entrepreneurship.htm
This site provides a helpful group of websites to teach kids about entrepreneurship.

Junior Achievement (JA)
http://www.ja.org
This is the Junior Achievement's home website. It describes the mission, purpose, and history of the organization. It gives real-life examples of the hands-on business experience children learn through JA.

YoungBiz
http://www.youngbiz.com
The website offers advice on each stage of developing a young person's business from getting it started to helping it grow. It also includes information on entrepreneur internships, camps, success stories, and more.

INDEX

ABOUT THE AUTHOR

Patricia J. Murphy makes her money by writing. She writes children's fiction and nonfiction books, early readers, and poetry. She also writes for magazines, corporations, museums, and children's book and educational publishers. She lives in the Chicago area.

PHOTO ACKNOWLEDGMENTS

The photographs in this book are reproduced with the permission of: Hypnoclips, pp, 6, 11, 13, 15, 30 (top), 31; © Alex Wong/Getty Images, p. 7; © Todd Strand/Independent Picture Service, pp. 8, 9 (both), 19 (lip balm courtesy of Beet Lips); courtesy of Maggie and Allie Cawood-Smith/Beet Lips, pp. 18, 24 (webpage and logo); courtesy of Elise and Evan Macmillan/Chocolate Farm, pp. 26, 27; courtesy of Mary Catherine Lindsay/Grasshopper Press, p. 30 (logo and photo); courtesy of Devon Green, p. 34. The illustrations on pp. 1, 4, 10, 14, 16, 21, 22, 23, 28, 29, 35, 41 are by Bill Hauser.

Front cover: Bill Hauser. Back cover: Hypnoclips (both).